I AM A GIANT PANDA

Steve Macleod

MEDIA ENHANCED BOOKS
AV²
BY WEIGL™
ADDED VALUE • AUDIO VISUAL

Go to **www.av2books.com,** and enter this book's unique code.

BOOK CODE

E 197126

AV² by Weigl brings you media enhanced books that support active learning.

AV² provides enriched content that supplements and complements this book. Weigl's AV² books strive to create inspired learning and engage young minds in a total learning experience.

Your AV² Media Enhanced books come alive with...

Audio
Listen to sections of the book read aloud.

Video
Watch informative video clips.

Embedded Weblinks
Gain additional information for research.

Try This!
Complete activities and hands-on experiments.

Key Words
Study vocabulary, and complete a matching word activity.

Quizzes
Test your knowledge.

Slide Show
View images and captions, and prepare a presentation.

... and much, much more!

Published by AV² by Weigl
350 5th Avenue, 59th Floor New York, NY 10118
Website: www.av2books.com www.weigl.com

Macleod, Steve.
Giant Panda / Steve Macleod.
    p. cm. -- (I am)
 ISBN 978-1-61690-756-3 (hardcover : alk. paper) -- ISBN 978-1-61690-763-1 (softcover : alk. paper)
1. Giant Panda--Juvenile literature. I. Title.
QL737.C27M239 2011
599.789--dc22

                    2010052411

Printed in the United States of America in North Mankato, Minnesota
1 2 3 4 5 6 7 8 9 0 15 14 13 12 11

052011
WEP 37500

Project Coordinator: Aaron Carr Art Director: Terry Paulhus

Weigl acknowledges Getty Images as the primary image supplier for this title.

I AM A GIANT PANDA

In this book, I will teach you about

- myself
- my food
- my home
- my family

and much more!

I am a giant panda.

I can fit in a person's hand when I am born.

I have fur that works
like a raincoat.

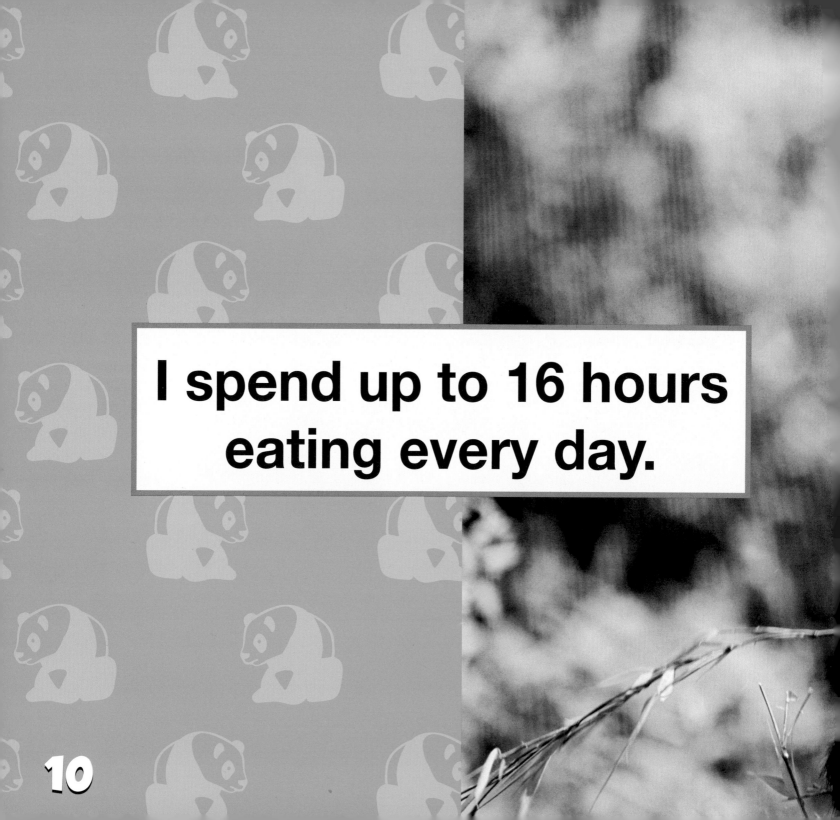

I spend up to 16 hours eating every day.

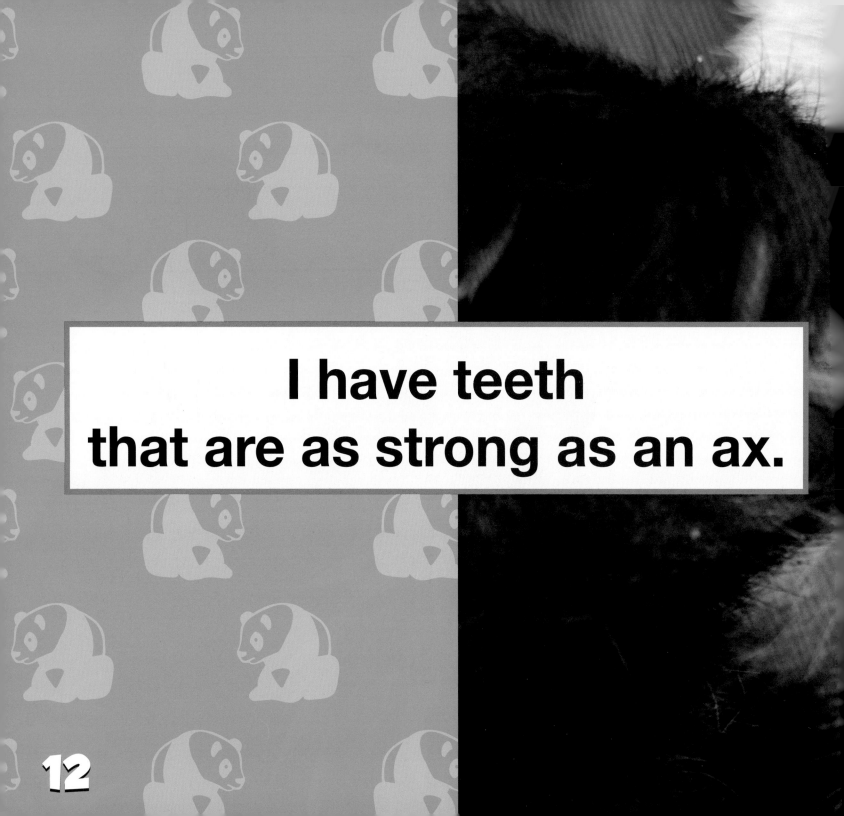

I have teeth
that are as strong as an ax.

12

13

I can peel and eat food
in less than one minute.

I hold my food
with all four paws.

I only sleep
four hours at a time.

19

I live in forests full of bamboo trees.

I am a giant panda.

20

GIANT PANDA FACTS

This page provides more detail about the interesting facts found in the book. Simply look for the corresponding page number to match the fact.

Pages 4-5

I am a giant panda. Giant pandas are sometimes called "panda bears." They have distinctive black and white fur. The white fur on their body and face stands out from their black limbs, ears, tail, and patches on their eyes.

Pages 6–7

Giant pandas can fit in a person's hand when they are born. Baby pandas weigh about 4 ounces (112 grams). A giant panda mother is 900 times larger than her baby when it is born. That is about the size difference between a hot air balloon and a grape.

Pages 8–9

Giant pandas have fur that works like a raincoat. There is a special oil on their fur to protect them from wet weather. This is important to help keep them warm and dry. There are many snowy and rainy days where giant pandas live.

Pages 10–11

Giant pandas spend up to 16 hours eating each day. During that time, a giant panda can eat 40 pounds (18 kilograms) of food, which is mostly bamboo. That is enough to feed an average person for more than a week.

Pages 12–13

Giant pandas have teeth that are as strong as an ax. These teeth are very sharp. Strong jaws also help giant pandas eat bamboo. This plant is so strong a person would have a hard time chopping through it with an ax.

Pages 14–15

Giant pandas can peel and eat food in less than one minute. They have an over-sized wrist bone that they use like a thumb. This helps giant pandas pick bamboo stalks and hold onto them while they peel the bamboo.

Pages 16–17

Giant pandas hold their food with all four paws. They need to get a good grip on their food to peel and eat it. Most of the time, a giant panda will eat sitting upright or lying on its back. This way, giant pandas can use all four paws to hold onto their food.

Pages 18–19

Giant pandas only sleep four hours at a time. When giant pandas are awake, they spend almost all of their time looking for food and eating. Then, they sleep for four hours before waking up and looking for food again.

Pages 20–21

Giant pandas live in forests full of bamboo trees. These forests are in China. Parts of China's bamboo forests are being cut down so people can live there. Giant pandas are now an endangered species. There are only 2,500 adult giant pandas left in nature.

WORD LIST

Research has shown that as much as 65 percent of all written material published in English is made up of 300 words. These 300 words cannot be taught using pictures or learned by sounding them out. They must be recognized by sight. This book contains 35 common sight words to help young readers improve their reading fluency and comprehension. This book also teaches young readers several important content words, such as proper nouns. These words are paired with pictures to aid in learning and improve understanding.

Page	Sight Words
4	a, am, I
6	a, am, can, hand, I, in, when
8	a, have, I, like, that, work
10	day, eat, every, I, to, up
12	an, are, as, have, I, that
14	and, can, eat, food, I, in, one, than
16	all, food, four, hold, I, my, with
18	a, at, four, I, only, sleep
20	a, am, full, I, in, live, of, tree

Page	Content Words
4	giant panda
6	born, fit, person
8	fur, raincoat
10	hour, spend
12	ax, strong, teeth
14	less, minute, peel
16	paw
18	hour, time
20	bamboo, forest, giant panda